Mountains form in many different ways.
They seem like they have been here forever and
will always be here, but over millions of years,
mountains come and go.

The older ones slowly crumble in the wind and rain, and wash away to the sea.

It happens so gradually that you can't see it.

NORTH AMERICA

SOUTH AMERICA

Mountains are
forming right now in
different places around the world.
The surface of the earth is like the cracked shell
of a hard-boiled egg. Large sections of land and
ocean are pieces of the earth's broken shell.

These pieces move
slowly, and sometimes they
rub and push against each other.
When this happens, it can make mountains.

What makes the pieces move, Momma?

The center of the earth is really hot. The rising heat moves the pieces very slowly, maybe the length of your big toe in one year. But sometimes they move a few feet in a sudden jolt. That's when you feel an earthquake!

Pieces of land can travel all the way around the world with tiny creeping movement over millions of years. For example, fossils of tropical plants and animals can be found in rocks that have traveled north to cold places like Alaska.

You can even find fossils of sea creatures at the tops of the tallest mountains.

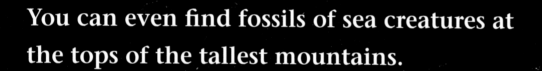

But why are the mountains so tall, Momma?

Some of the tallest
mountains grow where two
pieces of land smash together. The
land is crinkled, crunched, and folded,
kind of like how cars get crunched up
when they crash.

Something different happens where a piece of ocean bottom bumps into a piece of land. Because the ocean piece is heavier, it gets scrunched down under the land, similar to when you shove a spatula underneath a warm cookie.

The force of the shove melts the rock, creating fiery hot lava. It flows upward, squeezed from the earth like toothpaste from a tube.

The lava forms pointed
mountains called volcanoes.

Sometimes the pressure below is so strong, the top of the volcano is blown off. It is like how, if you step on a balloon, the pressure makes it pop.

When a volcano explodes, the air smells of stinky gases.

Mud and hot ash flow down the mountain.

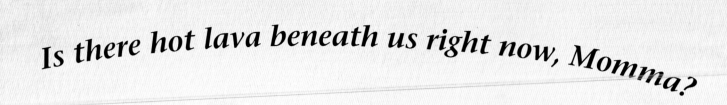

Is there hot lava beneath us right now, Momma?

There's only hot lava when a volcano is actively growing.

After a volcano stops growing, the melted rock still underneath it cools slowly into hard rock with large crystals.

Where else do mountains form, Momma?

Mountains can also form where a piece
of land is pulled in opposite directions by
forces within the earth. Rocks break, just like a
rubber band will break if you stretch it too far. The
broken blocks of land move against each other, and some
rise up to become mountains.

In Africa, there's a place where the land is
stretched almost completely apart. The low
valley may someday fill with seawater,
forming a new ocean.

Can mountains form in an ocean, Momma?

In a few places around the
world, hot melted rock rises to
the surface at a single spot, like
a water fountain. If the hot spot
is beneath an ocean, the
lava forms an island
mountain.

It was time to go home, but the girl had one more question.

Why does every mountain look different, Momma?

Every mountain is different, with a special past, just like every child. If you look closely at a mountain's rocks, you can discover its life story.

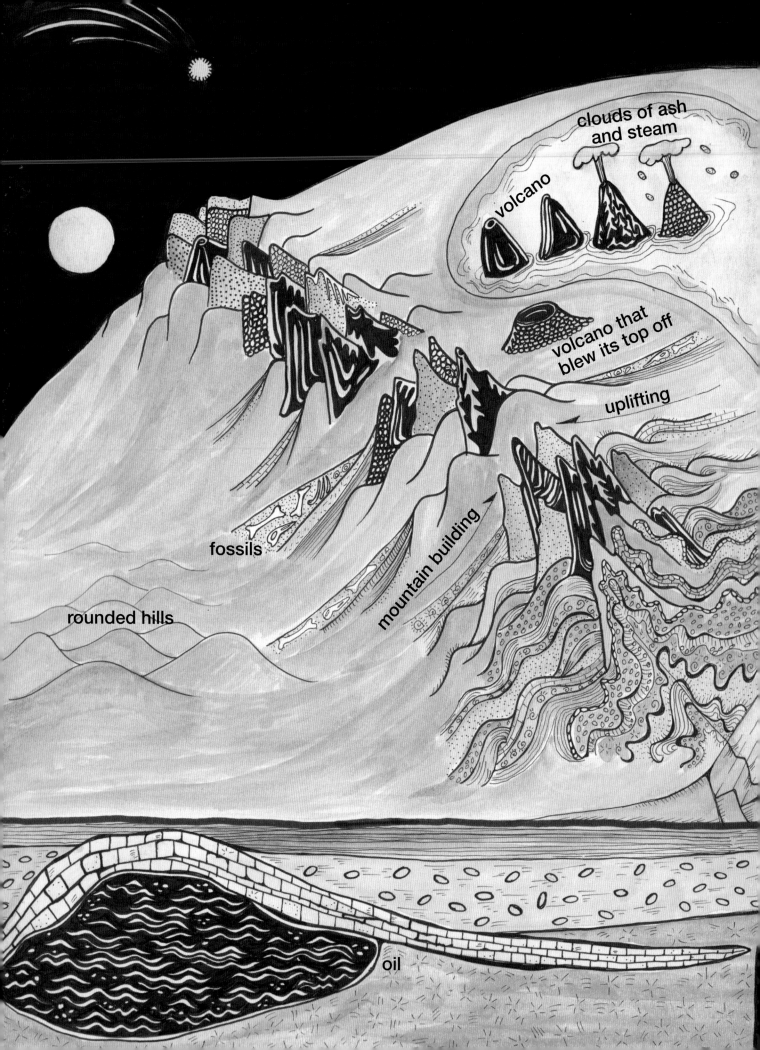

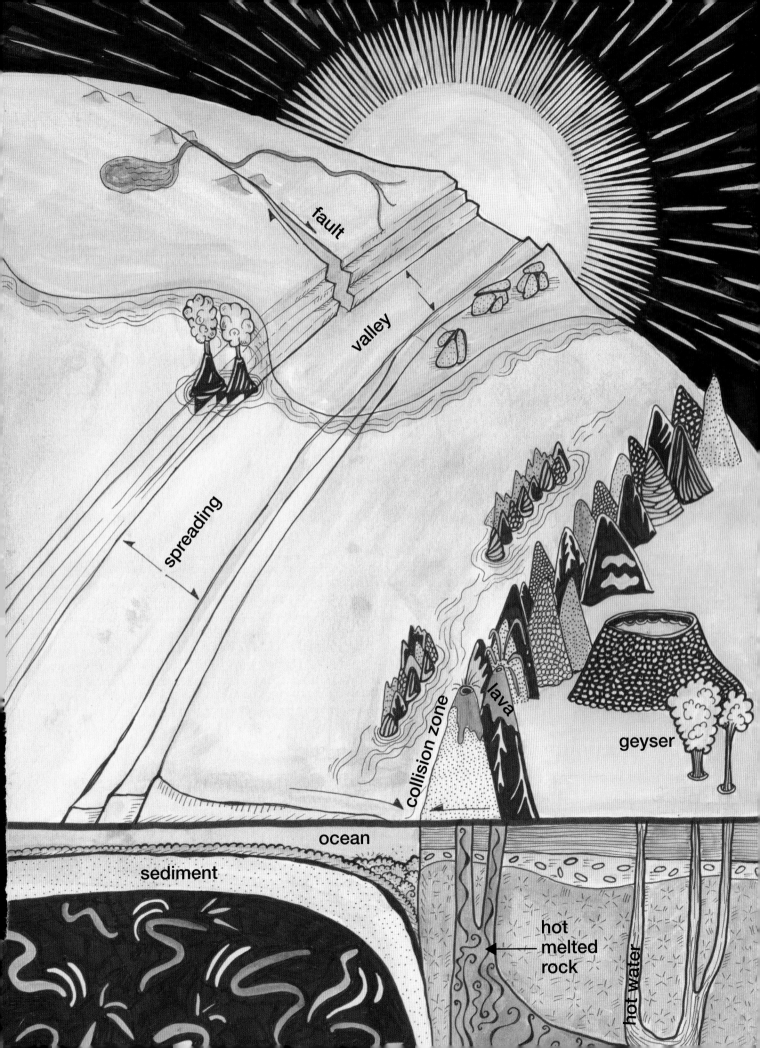

Stories of Real Mountains

Mount Katahdin is a mass of old granite in Maine. An enormous mountain range formed there when two pieces of land collided 400 million years ago. The continents are no longer cramming and shoving each other upward, and hot melted rock that formed deep below the mountains cooled into granite. Ice, water, and wind have removed the softer surrounding rock, exposing the hard granite.

Grand Teton in Wyoming rose along a fault, beginning about 9 million years ago, as North America was stretched. The mountain is one of the youngest in the Rocky Mountains and yet the stone that was launched upward is some of the oldest. Jackson Hole, the valley to its east, continues to sink.

Mount St. Helens in Washington is a volcano that is growing where a piece of ocean floor is colliding with North America. The volcano blew its top in 1980, creating a plume of ash over 12 miles high. An avalanche of mud flattened vegetation and buildings on the slope. A new dome of lava is forming today in the hole left behind by the explosion.

Mount Everest, the tallest peak in the world, is still rising as India collides with Asia. It is lifting skyward at a rate of almost 4 inches per year. The rocks of the majestic mountain are full of fossils of animals that lived in the sea.

Kilauea volcano on the island of Hawaii is forming above a hot spot. It is one of the most active volcanoes in the world today. The Hawaiian island chain stretches toward the northwest, tracing the path of the Pacific ocean floor as it moved over the hot spot. The islands are just the tops of lofty volcanic mountains that are mostly underwater.

Mount Kilimanjaro is a snow-covered mountain near the equator in Africa. It is part of a string of volcanoes that formed near the East African Rift Valley as Africa began to split apart. In the hills around the base of the volcano, coffee grows in the fertile volcanic soil.